T0198959

Aloha Cheerio

Judy Friesen-Wood

AuthorHouse™
1663 Liberty Drive
Bloomington, IN 47403
www.authorhouse.com
Phone: 833-262-8899

Because of the dynamic nature of the Internet, any web addresses or links contained in this book may have changed since publication and may no longer be valid. The views expressed in this work are solely those of the author and do not necessarily reflect the views of the publisher, and the publisher hereby disclaims any responsibility for them.

Any people depicted in stock imagery provided by Getty Images are models, and such images are being used for illustrative purposes only.
Certain stock imagery © Getty Images.

This book is printed on acid-free paper.

ISBN: 978-1-4634-3118-1 (sc)
ISBN: 978-1-4918-6095-3 (e)

Library of Congress Control Number: 2011910724

Print information available on the last page.

Published by AuthorHouse 12/07/2022

authorHOUSE®

Illustrated by: Anna Wood

She was a cute dog
and energetic too,

She would run and
jump looking for
something to do.

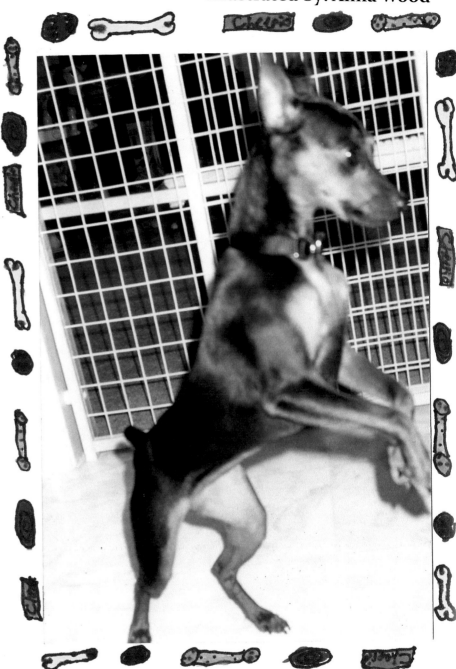

We found her in a newspaper ad
We went to meet her so I would not be sad.

We brought her into our home
If outside put her on a leash so she would not roam.

A name we must give
her, we never knew
which name
would stay,

One morning looking
at a cereal box we read
'Cheerio'
- she came right away.

Cheerio was a good dog and had lots of love to give,
Cheerio had finally found a home in which she would be safe
to live. Others had not been nice to her,
But now loving humans brushed her fur.

North Carolina is where she was born,
She liked her new home, of that she was not torn.

Missouri was her next home, she traveled in my truck.
When meal time was long in-between in her mouth
her food
dish was tucked.

She had her own area on a porch that was screened in,
She would sleep and play all day
– Oh how I loved my Min Pin!

9

Illustrated by: Anna Wood

From there we traveled to Hawaii in the cargo bin she flew,
Once there she went into quarantine I was so very blue.

Without her in the new house it was all so very quiet.
But in 30 days she was out and
we knew that she would love it.

We took her to the beach
in the country she could go,

We put her on a boogie board
with a life jacket
when the waves
were low.

12

She became a mommy of three there,
We kept one; we thought that would be fair.

13

She traveled then to Washington State,
She started with a cough which could have been her fate.

14

Back to Hawaii we chose to go,
She loved the warm weather so!

But her cough got worse and she had trouble breathing,
We tried with all our might to see where this was leading.

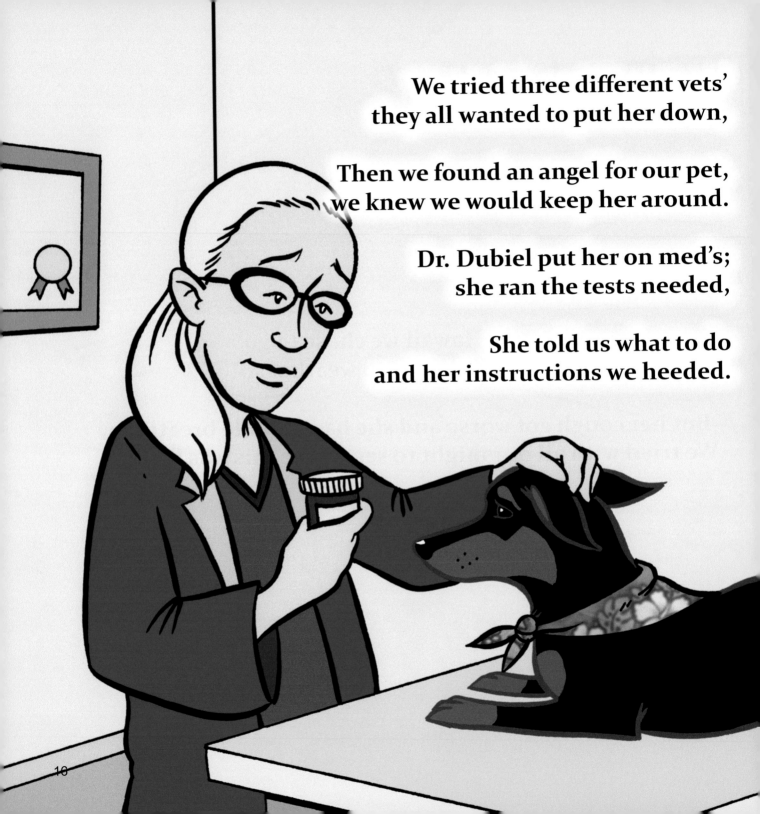

We tried three different vets'
they all wanted to put her down,

Then we found an angel for our pet,
we knew we would keep her around.

Dr. Dubiel put her on med's;
she ran the tests needed,

She told us what to do
and her instructions we heeded.

Four more years past
and more happy memories were gathered

But we saw her strength was going
and that was what mattered.

She slept a lot and had trouble getting around.
She didn't always eat and could not hear a sound.

17

Then it happened the day we didn't want to face,
Getting ready for a Vet visit she was found in a bad place.

We ran her to the Vet
but she had already gone,
She was in a better place now,
on that we could count on.

18

We remember her by talking;
we take time each day,

It seems we
each have a
good memory of her to say.

We write poems,
gather pictures,
think of her a lot,
We even think of places
that were her special spot.

Each day our sadness will get easier and our load lighter,
We will smile as we think of her and it will make our day
brighter.

We believe she is in Heaven and
we will see her again one day.

We believe she is joined
by those who have already gone that way,

She has lots of love and
can finally once again run and play.

We hope with our story told that
if you have lost a special friend,
Our book will help your heart to start to mend.
It will take some time and sad you will be,
But sweet memories and thoughts will let you see,

Your friend is somewhere safe and loved,
Waiting for you to join them
– with a hug!

Printed in the United States
by Baker & Taylor Publisher Services